GOLDEN GATE
NATIONAL PARKS

TEXT BY CHRISTINE COLASURDO

GOLDEN GATE NATIONAL PARKS CONSERVANCY, SAN FRANCISCO, CALIFORNIA

URBAN, WILD

IT'S A BREEZY MAY MORNING AT THE CONTINENT'S EDGE in northern California. The wind blows straight off the Pacific Ocean, over the heads of migrating dolphins, over sandstone cliffs where bank swallows nest, over acres of lupines whose swaying petals beckon hungry bees. It's a steady wind, a fat wind, as the hang gliders say, coming onshore from a velvet horizon of water and fog. On a high bluff, a hang glider stands face into the wind, his eyes on the ocean as a red-tailed hawk hunts above. Gripping the bar of his wing, he pauses to let the hawk pass. Then, with an energetic *hey!*, he runs five short steps and leaps off the cliff. The wind catches his wing's pink sail, and he rises north along the bluff like a child's lost balloon. Casting no shadow, the dark raptor flies south, its rufous tail splayed in the fog-soft air. Like the hang glider, it sails over 500,000-year-old sandstone that is slowly crumbling into the ocean, wildflowers and all. Then, as if to illustrate the force of wind as much as its agility as a predator, the bird hangs frozen in the sky, still as a snapshot. And then it plummets out of sight.

For hawk and hang glider, it's just another day in the Golden Gate National Parks. Just another day in a 118-square-mile complex of beaches, forests, headlands, and historic sites that frames San Francisco with the largest urban parklands in the world. Just another day in a wind-whipped, water-washed land where the rocks themselves announce: *Look out.* The earth beneath your feet is creeping north to Alaska. Or maybe it's tumbling in whole chunks into the ocean. It is time for wind in the face, time to unlearn everything you learned about *terra firma*. Time to read the land as the hawk reads it: in one fell swoop.

Point Bonita Lighthouse, first operational in 1855, was relocated to its current position in 1877; its second-order Fresnel light came to California from Paris on a ship around Cape Horn. (AL GREENING)

Red-tailed hawks are diligent hunters with a remarkable ability to acclimate themselves to the human world, a characteristic that helps make them successful Bay Area residents. (BARBARA SAMUELSON)

It won't be simple. Packed with superlatives, it is a land that makes descriptions seem exaggerated: Its rocks are among the most complicated bits of oceanic crust. Its plants and animals form one of the most species-rich regions on the continent. Its migrations range from tiny clouds of red ladybugs to acre-wide pods of gray whales. Its redwoods are among the tallest living things on the planet. And the ocean that laps against its shoreline is the largest and oldest on Earth.

It is also a land that defies categories. Its boundaries encompass a hodgepodge of federal, state, and special-district lands officially known as the Golden Gate National Recreation Area. Today, these parklands are unofficially and affectionately called the Golden Gate National Parks— a plural epithet that reflects the parklands' fragmented geography. This extraordinary mosaic of a park spreads across San Mateo, San Francisco, and Marin counties. At times it is easily accessed by asphalt; other times it is roadless and remote. Its 75,500 acres begin with the redwood canyons of the Phleger Estate in the south and continue north through the Presidio in San Francisco to the redwoods and ranchlands of northern Marin. Its 59 miles of coastline extend from the barnacled tidepools of the Fitzgerald Marine Reserve to the oyster-studded shores of Tomales Bay. The sum of these parts makes for one of the nation's largest coastal parks. And with more than 17 million people exploring the park each year, it is also one of the most frequently visited.

Like the geology of its rocks, the Golden Gate National Recreation Area is a collection of bits and pieces added slowly over time. The major thrust for a park began in the 1960s with the open-space dreams of local conservationists and U.S. Representative Phillip Burton. These dreams became law in 1972 when Congress set aside land for the park and gave it a name. The park's size doubled, then tripled, as the U. S. Army began to close its coastal defenses and conservationists argued for the military sites to become part of the park. Although the accretion has been mostly of former army lands, it has also been of former state and municipal lands, and occasionally of private donations, such as the park's oldest parcel, Muir Woods National Monument, which was given to the federal government in 1908 by William and Elizabeth Kent. Even today the park continues to grow, parcel by parcel, with 7 distinct watersheds and 19 separate ecosystems. Out of this mostly unforeseen, sometimes fought-over, and hugely fortuitous process has evolved a collage of natural and cultural sites that tell a long story, a 10,000-year-old human story that begins with the ancestral villages of the region's native people and continues today with historic forts, an infamous prison, a celebrated waterfront, and a rust-colored bridge that connects the northern parklands to the south and is the most walked-upon and photographed in the world.

Hang gliders flock to Fort Funston to take advantage of its brisk ocean winds as well as a launch site built especially for the gliders' use.
(KERRICK JAMES)

But to dwell upon superlatives is to miss the intimate interplay that renders the Golden Gate so alluring: its black rocks lathered by frothy saltwater; oak-filled draws amid tawny headlands; ocean swells punctured by anchovy-seeking pelicans; glistening skins of barking sea lions; solitary paths winding their way toward hilltops; curling cascades of fog through wind-gnarled trees. It is when a brisk breeze rips the fog off ridges and the sun warms your face that the land's magnificence leaps out at you, a magnificence fashioned by the collision of continent and ocean, longitude and latitude, human whim and weather, sea and salt air. You don't need anyone to report on superlatives. Like the hang glider, you are there.

NORTH OF THE GOLDEN GATE

THE NATIONAL PARKLANDS NORTH OF THE GOLDEN GATE stretch for more than forty miles, farther than most humans could walk in a day, and yet a red-tailed hawk could fly over them in a few hours. With an average wingspan of four feet and an ability to travel a hundred miles a day, a migrating red-tail could fly from Tomales Bay to the Golden Gate Bridge and hardly stop to rest. In its journey, it would traverse some of the least-developed land near San Francisco—untamed land that came from the ocean, borders the ocean, and is still being shaped and reclaimed by the ocean. The red-tail knows this in its own way: it rides the updrafts from onshore breezes, preys on gopher snakes in the wind-bald hills, and senses instinctively that although it can continue its journey south, east, or north, it cannot go west: not over open water. What seems like an endless grand Pacific to humans is a water-wall to a hawk.

And so the red-tail lingers—along with other hawks, falcons, and eagles—in a breeze-burnished, rodent-rich country of high ridges hemmed by bay and ocean. This lingering, particularly apparent in autumn, contributes to one of the greatest hawk migrations in North America. From September to December, volunteer observers with the Golden Gate Raptor Observatory in the Marin Headlands have counted as many as 36,000 birds of prey. With nineteen species of migrating and resident raptors darkening the skies, the hawk-dappled headlands offer visitors a rare glimpse into the odd ecological coupling of water and hawk.

A dizzying sweep of international-orange cable bisects the fabled Golden Gate. On the bay side is Fort Baker, a former army post; on the ocean side, the Marin Headlands rise up from the sea. (DAVID SANGER)

Or perhaps it is ultimately a coupling of hawk and plate tectonics—that age-old rearranging of the Earth's jigsaw-puzzle crust. For it is the 200-million-year-old bumping of plates that has created the crumpled topography where the hawks converge. If not for creeping crustal plates, there would be neither bay nor beaches, neither hills nor headlands, perhaps not even fog. There would be only open ocean, as there was until roughly 13 million years ago. Around that time, the rocks of the Coast Range—squeezed upward by slowly colliding plates—began to poke their way out of the water. This plate collision could not be made plainer than by the red-tail's hypothetical journey from Tomales Bay toward the Golden Gate. In its brief flight, the hawk would fly over part of one of the world's most active geological faults: the San Andreas. Extending from Baja to northern California, this 750-mile-long fault is just one in a massive system of faults that marks the collision boundary of the continental North American Plate and the oceanic Pacific Plate. In southern California, the San Andreas Fault appears as far inland as Joshua Tree National Park. But in the Bay Area it happens to run roughly between land and ocean, and shapes much of the Golden Gate National Recreation Area.

The northern parklands display exquisite evidence of the plates' slow-motion crash—from major landmarks to pebbles held in the palm of one's hand. In some places, the fault's pulverized rock has eroded into watery depressions such as Tomales Bay. In the Olema Valley, the fault created sag ponds and cow pastures that jumped several feet during the 1906 earthquake. At Hawk Hill in the Marin Headlands, a hunting red-tail might cast its shadow upon road cuts that expose the tectonically pressed rocks. All along Conzelman Road you can see red, twisted rock known as chert, which began on the ocean floor 150 million years ago and was later scraped off onto North America as a series of oceanic plates slid under the continent and melted beneath it. The skeletons of tiny sea creatures called radiolarians are entombed in the chert. A few miles from the road cuts, you can walk to Point Bonita Lighthouse and stand upon pillow basalt, another ocean-floor rock that was plastered onto the continent through plate movement.

The basalt and chert are only two in a mixture of Franciscan rocks that make up much of the Coast Range of northern California. These igneous, metamorphic, and sedimentary rocks create a varied foundation for the park's terrestrial animals and plants, such as the coast redwoods, whose ancestral species dominated the region for millions of years. The fog-loving redwoods have receded as California has become settled and its climate drier. With its 1,000-year-old trees, Muir Woods National Monument preserves a tiny yet towering vestige of the vast forests of *Sequoia sempervirens* that once flourished. Alongside the forests have evolved plant communities that require less moisture, such as coastal scrub, oak woodlands, grasslands, and chaparral. Still other plants, including exotic invaders like French broom and fennel, have arrived through ranching, army plantings, and other human activities. Along with dune and riparian areas, the northern parklands offer a kaleidoscope of habitats for species with different needs, from the saltwater-loving limpet to the fire-loving manzanita. As a result, visitors can experience an abundant array of wildlife throughout the seasons as well as several different vegetation communities during one brief hike. In the Olema Valley, for instance, the Randall Trail starts on the valley's grassy floor and climbs two miles through Douglas-firs to the redwood-shaded crest of Bolinas Ridge. Near Tennessee Valley, the Oakwood Trail begins in a shady canyon of coast live oak and ends two miles later in sun-warmed coastal scrub. And in the Marin Headlands, a five-mile loop of the Miwok, Wolf Ridge, and Coastal trails takes hikers through wetlands, coastal scrub, and wildflower meadows to end at fine-peb-

These weather-beaten barns are testimony to Olema Valley's ranching past.
(LARRY ULRICH)

bled Rodeo Beach. Perhaps the most stunning hike, however, is the half-mile walk to Point Bonita Lighthouse. Built in 1855, the lighthouse still warns ships away from the rocky coast. Here, quite literally, visitors cross a chasm separating land from sea.

The northern parklands also provide significant swaths of protected habitat for many of the park's 80 sensitive, rare, threatened, and endangered species. Near Martinelli Ranch, great egrets spear fish in Tomales Bay. In Muir Woods, coho salmon and steelhead trout spawn in Redwood Creek. In Rodeo Lagoon, a small fish called the tidewater goby thrives in brackish waters. In the Marin Headlands, mission blue butterflies feed on lupines. At Bird Island, great flocks of brown pelicans and Brandt's cormorants fill the air. And at night, while hawks and shorebirds roost, ten species of rare bats wheel and dive for insects, and three species of rare owls sweep the parklands on silent wings.

Such open, animal-rich country in the densely populated Bay Area originates partly from Marin County's ranching and dairying past, where large pockets of land were left unbuilt during rapid twentieth-century development. This farming tradition continues today through leased parklands in Olema Valley. But the wild land is also a legacy of the army, whose defenses, such as Fort Cronkhite's Nike Missile Site, remain anchored in the landscape as sobering reminders of an earlier time. The army's legacy also includes historic buildings that today house such organizations as the Marine Mammal Center, the Headlands Center for the Arts, and the Bay Area Discovery Museum. As a consequence, the northern parklands are celebrated daily by such people as animal rescuers taking care of seals, artists translating the landscape into paint and canvas, and children singing songs even as red-tailed hawks drift by overhead, quiet as incoming fog.

In the past, Redwood Creek, which runs through Muir Woods and empties into the Pacific at Muir Beach, had a healthy annual salmon run, but years of environmental degradation reduced their numbers. Restoration is a high priority here. (LARRY ULRICH)

The beach primrose is a plant with a mission—this day-blooming perennial forms large mats that give stability to plant and insect communities in the park's coastal strand.
(CHARLES KENNARD)

Pull-outs along Conzelman Road in the Marin Headlands provide visitors with one of the most popular views of the Golden Gate Bridge.
(INGER HOGSTROM)

The Pacific treefrog, shown here clinging to watercress with its sticky toe pads, is most often found near fresh water.
(CHARLES KENNARD)

Aside from being beautiful places to visit, the parks also serve Bay Area schools as glorious outdoor classrooms. Children participate in ranger-led programs, learn about birds of prey, and build—and test paddle—tule boats.

(TL: BRENDA THARP; TR: DAVID JESUS; BR: CHARLES KENNARD)

A blur of color, this cyclist is on his way north across the Golden Gate Bridge, a breathtaking ride. (KERRICK JAMES)

Rising from the surf just off the Marin Coast, these mounds of pillow basalt—popularly known as "sea stacks"—are evidence of long-ago volcanic activity deep beneath the ocean floor. (GALEN ROWELL)

California quail skitter through the underbrush and perch on fence posts in the park's northern coastal canyons and valleys; walkers on the Tennessee Valley Trail are often treated to sightings of these gregarious birds with their black, forward-curving topknots.
(BRENDA THARP)

Northern California surfing requires a wetsuit; with water temperatures hovering around 56 degrees and fast-moving currents, surfing off the Marin Coast is exciting but not for amateurs.
(BRENDA THARP)

Native Douglas iris begins blooming in early February in areas as diverse as Muir Woods' redwood forest and the Marin Headlands' coastal prairie regions. (CHARLES KENNARD)

The *Boletus satanus*, or Devil's boletus, which is considered to be poisonous, is found only in California under stands of oaks in autumn and early winter. (CHARLES KENNARD)

Horsetails (right), an ancient plant essentially unchanged except in size from the days of the dinosaur, and bee plant (left) are common sights in the Muir Woods riparian community. (CHARLES KENNARD)

This tightly wrapped California poppy will open to its full extent during the course of the day and close up at night. A native species, it occupies many ecological niches. (ROY EISENHARDT)

Blue lupine, often interspersed with California poppies, turn the coastal hills and prairies a striking violet-blue in early spring. (BRENDA THARP)

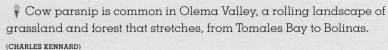 Cow parsnip is common in Olema Valley, a rolling landscape of grassland and forest that stretches, from Tomales Bay to Bolinas. (CHARLES KENNARD)

Beach strawberry, once a food source for the region's native people, is an important member of the coastal dune community. (CHARLES KENNARD)

Fog at dawn over Muir Woods. The fog, which is drawn inland by heat in interior valleys, provides much of the moisture needed by trees and other vegetation during the long, dry California summer and fall. (BRENDA THARP)

The peregrine falcon, a cliff-nesting raptor, is an extremely long-winged bird that has adapted to city life. Their nests have been found tucked into recesses of tall buildings and on bridge support beams. (DAVID JESUS)

Nike Missile Site SF-88 in the Marin Headlands, restored and maintained largely by volunteers, is the only place where the Cold War is interpreted. (AL GREENING)

Habitat preservation and restoration are two vital park activities, especially for the survival of species like the endangered mission blue butterfly, which prefers silvery blue lupine as a host for its eggs.

(EMILY NEWBY)

Raccoons are frequent nocturnal visitors to the parks' rubbish bins. Though their masked faces are irresistibly cute, they can wreak havoc with campers' unprotected food supplies. (AL GREENING)

For most of the year, fog advances and retreats regularly through the Golden Gate as ocean currents are pushed down the coast. Frigid water from far below the surface rises to the top, chills the sea air, and produces the fog that rolls down the Marin hills and blankets the bay. (BRENDA THARP)

At the end of the two-mile-long, wide, and well-groomed Tennessee Valley Trail is Tennessee Cove; both are named for the SS *Tennessee*, whose shipwrecked remains lie under the ocean surf. (BRENDA THARP)

Hikers on Muir Woods' Bootjack or Fern Creek trails in late autumn are likely to encounter ladybugs en masse; the orange-and-black beetles migrate to these cool spots from inland valleys. In late winter, the ladybugs mate and then return to their previous homes to lay eggs and die. (JED MANWARING)

At Rodeo Beach, solitary contemplation of ocean waves is one of several popular activities. (GALEN ROWELL)

Tennessee Valley has known the beat of horse hooves for centuries. Modern-day equestrians follow paths once familiar to native people, Spanish explorers, U.S. Army soldiers, and ranchers. (BRENDA THARP)

Ghosts of coastal defense batteries linger in the fog; mounts for the big cannon used through WWII stud the Marin Headlands. (ROB BADGER)

In the Headlands, geology is a tangible factor of daily life. Here, where the edge of North America meets the Pacific Ocean, drop-offs are common. (AL GREENING)

Ribbons of red chert, folded and uplifted, can be seen from the car window on a drive up Conzelman Road above the Golden Gate Bridge. The Marin Headlands provide textbook examples of northern California geology. (BRENDA THARP)

Moonrise over the Golden Gate Bridge (opposite). The Headlands' dark mass creates a dramatic counterpoint to the bridge's upswept towers. (DAVID SANGER)

Muir Woods is home to a small population of northern spotted owls, who prefer complex and usually old-growth forest environments. (CHARLES KENNARD)

Muir Woods' damp, low-light conditions provide a perfect environment for fungi such as this oyster mushroom, which grows on rotting logs. (CHARLES KENNARD)

Stinson Beach—a smooth, white crescent—is one of the Golden Gate National Parks' few "swimming" beaches. This three-mile-long sandbar has been popular with local residents for more than a century. (MINDY MANVILLE)

SOUTH OF THE GOLDEN GATE

NOTHING IS LOST ON A RED-TAILED HAWK soaring over San Francisco Bay. Having braved a water crossing, it senses the possibility of its next meal in the brushy slopes of Angel Island, or even Alcatraz Island, with its somber cellhouse and skittering mice. According to Buzz Hull of the Golden Gate Raptor Observatory, a red-tailed hawk once nabbed a pigeon out of San Francisco's crowded Union Square. So the paved and pedestrian-filled reaches of the southern parklands pose no particular impediment to one of North America's largest and most common species of hawk. Throughout the park, the opportunistic red-tail chases its shadow over buildings as well as beaches, over forts as well as forests, over streets as well as streams.

If a red-tail were to continue its southbound journey through the park, it would encounter land whose wild and metropolitan features are so tightly interwoven that it is impossible to separate them. At Alcatraz, for instance, it would sweep over the park's darkest ruins of civilization and its liveliest colonies of nesting birds. It would then veer toward land, where it would ascend above Fort Mason, whose vibrant museums border the last remnant of undeveloped bay shore in all of San Francisco. It might then follow the shoreline westward, scanning Crissy Field for gophers even as cars speed toward the Golden Gate Bridge. Then it would fly over Fort Point, over serpentine outcrops with rare wildflowers, and weave its way through the Presidio, where Lobos Creek—the city's last free-flowing stream—gurgles past roads. It might then head

South of the Golden Gate, the Presidio's green mass gradually emerges out of San Francisco's dense streetscape. (BARON WOLMAN)

west, around Lands End, to rest for a moment at Sutro Heights. There, it would perch above waves licking away the concrete ruins of the once-extravagant Sutro Baths.

Such contrasting scenery is the outcome of thousands of years of human activity in and around the park. Beginning with the *Yelamu* people, who once hunted elk and grizzly bears in what is now San Francisco, the Golden Gate has been inhabited for centuries. Thought to be a subgroup of the Ohlone, the Yelamu enjoyed an abundance of shellfish, game, and edible plants year-round in the mild climate. But their way of life was forever altered when the Spanish began settling the area in 1776. The Spanish subjugated the California tribes, and brought cattle and European seeds that dramatically affected the region's vegetation. Then Mexican and eventually American homesteaders arrived, and hunted the elk and grizzlies to local extinction. The new inhabitants also cut down oaks and redwoods, diverted creeks, filled in the bay's shore, and planted exotic trees such as eucalyptus, Monterey cypress, and Monterey pine. Most of the park's exotic trees were planted beginning in the late nineteenth century by Mayor Adolph Sutro and the U. S. Army, who both hoped to "beautify" the treeless, windswept dunes that characterized the Yelamu's original environs. The army also cultivated South African iceplant and European dune grass, which crowded out native wildflowers such as beach morning-glory and seaside daisy.

Today, with the transfer of the army's holdings to the National Park Service, the Golden Gate National Recreation Area is no longer so much a place of development and defense as it is one of recreation and restoration. Human activities in the park have shifted from building military forts to rebuilding native-plant communities. Guns have been replaced by garden shovels, army access roads have become hiking trails, and hilltop observers now search the ocean for whales instead of warships. In some areas, the park is actually wilder than it was fifty years ago.

The parklands south of the Golden Gate illustrate how people are working to return the land to a more biologically diverse condition. In one of the country's largest and most sophisticated volunteer efforts on national parklands, thousands of volunteers have pulled weeds and replanted hundreds of acres with native wildflowers, shrubs, and trees. Degraded portions of Crissy Field, the Presidio, Fort Funston, Milagra Ridge, and Sweeney Ridge have been transformed into flower-laden dunes, a tidal marsh, and hillsides blooming with yarrow, Indian paintbrush, and lizardtail. Together with restored sites in the northern parklands, the southern half of the park is being tended to enrich its flora and fauna, so that species like the endangered Presidio manzanita and threatened red-legged frog might survive. The restored hillsides also offer human visitors the fragrances and textures of wilder times, when the Yelamu walked the land and spoke a language now almost lost.

The southern parklands demonstrate how the park is not only a garden of stewardship but a splendid place to play. The large and diverse population residing near the park experiences it in vastly different ways. At Ocean Beach it is fished and surfed; at Thornton Beach it is galloped upon by horses and flown over by paragliders; at Fort Point it is dipped by crab pots; along Sweeney Ridge it is perused by birders and botanists; at Crissy Field it is enjoyed by dog-walkers and kite-fliers; and throughout the Presidio it is lived in and studied by urban naturalists and schoolchildren alike.

For a red-tailed hawk, it is a place of wind. It is an eolian place where even on a day when sails lag and rocks bake in the sun, the cypresses and pines lean away from the ocean, remembering the force of each gust in their branches. It is a place where hardly any effort is needed for a hawk to ride an afternoon breeze from the Cliff House to the park's southern reaches, where part of the San Andreas Fault comes on land. There, near Thornton Beach, the fault veers inland as it heads south, traveling across Sweeney and Milagra ridges. Within a matter of miles, it slices through the park's southernmost tract: the Phleger Estate, a 1,200-acre forest where the quiet pools of Union Creek are dimpled by steelhead trout and dragonflies.

Just south of Thornton Beach, as the sun of the summer solstice drops into the ocean, several brown pelicans settle down for the night atop Mussel Rock, where the San Andreas Fault hits the shore. The large seabirds cast no shadow as they circle about the black sea stack, choosing a roost. Come winter solstice, they'll mostly be gone, flying south to Baja. A red-tailed hawk is also roosting quietly in a cypress tree, high up on the bluff. Come winter solstice, it too may disappear south, to Mexico or beyond. But it might just as easily swing north and stay, its shadow racing over ridges on fogless days, its harsh call announcing its satisfaction with such a conundrum of seacoast that is both wind-beaten and -blessed, ocean-born and -eroded, intensely urban and yet distinctly wild.

Foundation ruins filled with seawater are reminders of Adolph Sutro's fabulous baths—a 25,000-person facility with saltwater swimming pools regularly flushed by the tides, 517 private dressing rooms, restaurants, and arcades, all enclosed by 100,000 square feet of glass. During its heyday in the early 20th century, it was the largest of its type in the world. (BRENDA THARP)

The Golden Gate Promenade extends from Aquatic Park to the Golden Gate Bridge. One of its particularly beautiful stretches is through the newly restored Crissy Field area. Walking toward the city on a moonlit evening—the marsh on one side, the bay on the other, and the San Francisco skyline on the horizon—is a relaxing pastime for the city's residents and visitors alike. (DAVID SANGER)

Barn swallows, with their deeply forked tails and iridescent black and coppery cinnamon bodies, prefer to build their mud-daub nests on vertical, man-made surfaces. (GARY KRAMER)

Though the Presidio is square in the heart of one of California's most densely populated areas, ranger-led programs provide visitors with a traditional National Park experience. (CHARLES KENNARD)

Penitentiary inmates working in Alcatraz's New Industries building between 1941 and 1963 would not have seen Transamerica Pyramid's distinctive shape when they looked through this window. (AL GREENING)

A large, heavy seabird, the brown pelican is a common sight along the San Francisco coastline. Groups of pelicans often glide in loose formation, necks pulled into S-curves and powerful wings scarcely moving. (GARY KRAMER)

Milagra Ridge, once home to Nike missiles, is now a butterfly haven, supplying critically important habitat for the mission blue and San Bruno elfin species. The NPS closely monitors recreational use of this area on the species' behalf. The plants in the foreground, pearly everlasting, thrive in northern California's coast ranges. (CHARLES KENNARD)

Until Adolph Sutro bought the property, landscaped it, and opened it to the public, the area now known as Sutro Heights was a lonely expanse of wind-blown bluff overlooking the ocean. (BRENDA THARP)

Between 1969 and 1971, Native American civil rights activists occupied Alcatraz Island; they left behind numerous examples of "Red Power" graffiti. (AL GREENING)

Symmetrical rows of grave markers march across a gentle rise in the Presidio's National Cemetery. Buffalo Soldiers, Medal of Honor winners, and Union spies are among those buried here. (DAVID SANGER)

A weatherbeaten marker atop Sweeney Ridge commemorates the location from which Spanish explorers first saw San Francisco Bay. (AL GREENING)

The cellhouse on Alcatraz—abandoned by the Bureau of Prisons in 1963—is a place of shadows and echoes. (ROB BADGER)

Small "penthouses" protected the opening to Fort Point's stairways; they also provided shelter for those on sentry duty atop the fort's walls. (DAVID SANGER)

The ghostly shape of the Presidio forest softened by fog gives a somber aura to the West Coast Memorial to the Missing of World War II. Though the Presidio is now national parkland, for over a century and a half, it existed to serve the country's military needs. (GALEN ROWELL)

The Presidio's Baker Beach is a favorite fishing spot for city-dwellers. The Golden Gate National Parks give local residents plenty of venues to escape crowds and traffic.
(AL GREENING)

An explosion of shorebirds erupts from the water's edge in a whir of wings and movement. The parks provide a belt of protected coastal interface that extends fifty-nine miles north to south and offers shelter and feeding opportunities for numerous bird species.
(GARY KRAMER)

The endangered San Francisco garter snake (*Thamnophis sirtalis tetrataenia*) is a protected denizen of the parks' watershed lands in San Mateo County. (DENNIS SHERIDAN)

The Presidio's Interfaith Chapel is decorated with a mural representing three cultures whose histories are tightly interwoven with that of the post. (DAVID SANGER)

Beach walking is enjoyed by many, and the Golden Gate National Parks provide opportunities for the activity, both north and south of the bridge. (DAVID SANGER)

Alcatraz, directly in line with the Golden Gate, was home to the West Coast's first operational lighthouse (1854). Today's lighthouse is the island's second, built to replace the smaller structure that was overshadowed by the construction of the massive cellhouse—completed in 1912—on the island's crest. (JEFF GNASS)

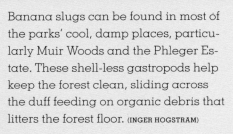

Banana slugs can be found in most of the parks' cool, damp places, particularly Muir Woods and the Phleger Estate. These shell-less gastropods help keep the forest clean, sliding across the duff feeding on organic debris that litters the forest floor. (INGER HOGSTRAM)

Great egrets are a common sight in the parks' wetland areas. These stately white birds assume this pose when hunting. (GARY KRAMER)

The tussock moth larvae, shown here on an arroyo willow leaf, periodically causes serious damage to stands of western conifers; the colorful larval body hairs can irritate human skin, causing an itching rash. (CHARLES KENNARD)

The rich system of blood vessels in jack rabbits' long ears helps regulate the rabbits' internal temperature, (DAVID SANGER)

Anemones thrive in the tidepools on Alcatraz's western edge. The tidepools were created in the late nineteenth and early twentieth centuries, when the army cut down parts of the island and pushed the debris over the edge. (ROY EISENHARDT)

California sea lions are common along the parks' rocky shoreline and near shore waters. (MACDUFF EVERTON)

People are often surprised to discover that large predators such as coyotes survive and thrive in the Marin Headlands as well as in the watershed lands to the south. (GARY KRAMER)

The Presidio is a veritable museum of two hundred years of architectural styles. These red-brick barracks on Montgomery Street date from about the 1890s. (BRENDA THARP)

With Alcatraz as a backdrop, a board sailor skims across the bay. The waters off Crissy Field's East Beach are some of the most popular in the region for boardsailing. (ROY EISENHARDT)

Fort Mason's Great Meadow was once covered by rows and rows of military warehouses; after the creation of Golden Gate National Recreation Area in 1972, they were removed and the area was reclaimed as a green space. (BRENDA THARP)

When the Peninsula Open Space Trust acquired the Phleger Estate in San Mateo County and turned it over to the National Park Service, they saved a stand of second-growth redwoods and helped complete an approximately twenty-mile-long habitat corridor. (BRENDA THARP)

The wind under his wings, this hang glider soars out over the Pacific Ocean from Fort Funston's launching platform. The cliffs in the background are used seasonally as nesting sites by bank swallows. (BRENDA THARP)

For years, soldiers in gun emplacements like the one shown here watched for attacks that never came. Coastal defense fortifications stud the parks' Pacific coastline from north to south. (BRENDA THARP)

Built on a bluff cut down to almost water level in the 1850s, Fort Point was one of three forts planned by the army to defend the entrance to the bay. By the time it became obsolete after the Civil War, its guns had never been fired. When the Golden Gate Bridge was built in the mid-1930s, engineers redesigned the south anchorage to preserve the fort, which is considered to be one of the West Coast's finest examples of the brickmason's art. (BRENDA THARP)

🪶 Thousands of accipiters, such as this sharp-shinned hawk, migrate over park lands in the autumn.
[DAVID JESUS]

🦅 Cool, dim rooms at Fort Point echo with the sounds of long-gone soldiers. The brickwork vaulting is unusual for San Francisco-area buildings of the era. (CHARLES KENNARD)

◄ Native dune grasses bend in the wind at Crissy Field; the grasses represent just a tiny fraction of the native plants that were individually planted by hand during the area's restoration between 1998 and 2001.

(DAVID SANGER)

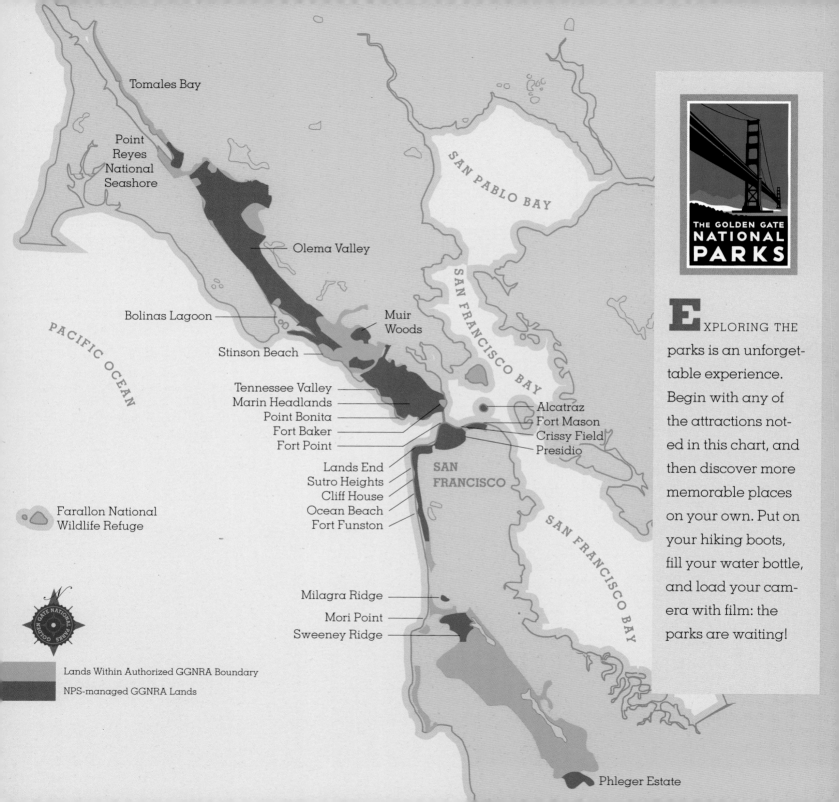

Tomales Bay

Point
Reyes
National
Seashore

Olema Valley

PACIFIC OCEAN

Bolinas Lagoon

Stinson Beach

Muir
Woods

Tennessee Valley
Marin Headlands
Point Bonita
Fort Baker
Fort Point

Farallon National
Wildlife Refuge

Lands End
Sutro Heights
Cliff House
Ocean Beach
Fort Funston

SAN PABLO BAY

SAN FRANCISCO BAY

Alcatraz
Fort Mason
Crissy Field
Presidio

SAN
FRANCISCO

SAN FRANCISCO BAY

Milagra Ridge

Mori Point

Sweeney Ridge

Lands Within Authorized GGNRA Boundary

NPS-managed GGNRA Lands

Phleger Estate

THE GOLDEN GATE
NATIONAL
PARKS

EXPLORING THE
parks is an unforget-
table experience.
Begin with any of
the attractions not-
ed in this chart, and
then discover more
memorable places
on your own. Put on
your hiking boots,
fill your water bottle,
and load your cam-
era with film: the
parks are waiting!

OLEMA VALLEY

General information: 415.464.5100

STINSON BEACH

General information: 415.868.1922

MUIR WOODS

General information: 415.388.2595

GETTING THERE

Highway 1 north skirts the valley's western edge and leads to Point Reyes Station at the valley's northernmost end. Or, from eastern Marin, take Sir Francis Drake Highway north through Samuel P. Taylor State Park; follow the highway as it turns west toward Point Reyes Station.

Highway 1 north runs along the coastline. Watch for signs directing you to the town of Stinson Beach and to the beach itself.

Highway 101 to Highway 1, then take Panoramic Highway; watch for signs directing you to Muir Woods National Monument.

Adult visitors pay a nominal entrance fee.

LOOK FOR

- Historic dairy ranches
- Point Reyes National Seashore
- Valley floor and ridgeline trails

- Audubon Canyon Ranch
- Bolinas Lagoon
- Stinson Beach

- Muir Beach
- Muir Woods
- Native plant nursery
- Redwood Creek

ACTIVITIES

Hiking, biking, birdwatching, wildflowers (in season); equestrian

Beachwalking, swimming, surfboarding, boardsailing, kayaking

Hiking, birdwatching, ranger-led programs

TIPS

The San Andreas Fault travels through the center of the valley and creates a number of interesting examples of fault topography, including parallel creeks flowing in opposite directions (Olema and Pine Gulch creeks).

Nearby Bolinas Lagoon is a good kayaking spot. In the spring, look for harbor seal pups, but keep your distance.

Muir Woods is within the Redwood Creek Watershed and is home to a number of threatened and endangered species.

	PARK	**GETTING THERE**	**LOOK FOR**	**ACTIVITIES**	**TIPS**

TENNESSEE VALLEY

General information: 415.331.1540

Getting There: Take Shoreline Highway to Tennessee Valley Road and the parking lot/trailhead near the Miwok Stables.

Look For:
- Tennessee Beach
- Remains of the SS *Tennessee* (visible at low tide)
- Lagoon shaded by a stand of eucalyptus
- Native plant nursery

Activities: Hiking, biking, birdwatching, beachwalking, picnicking, equestrian

Tips: The Tennessee Valley Trail is a perfect place for an easy walk with children—on foot, in strollers, or on small bicycles—and its surface makes it accessible for those using wheelchairs.

MARIN HEADLANDS

General information: 415.331.1540

Getting There: Highway 101 to the Alexander Avenue exit; go west on Conzelman Road (for picture book views of the Golden Gate Bridge and city skyline) or continue on Alexander Avenue to the intersection with Bunker Road. Watch for signs directing you to the Marin Headlands Visitor Center.

Look For:
- Hawk Hill
- Kirby Cove
- Native plant nursery
- Nike Missile, Battery Townsley, and other military-era sites
- Point Bonita Lighthouse
- Rodeo Lagoon and Beach

Activities: Overnight camping, hiking, biking, birdwatching (raptors and shorebirds), wildflowers and whalewatching (in season), equestrian, ranger-led programs

Tips: The Marin Headlands provide a dramatic setting for a number of nonprofit organizations with environmental and/or creative missions; many are open to the public. For more information, inquire at the Visitor Center.

ALCATRAZ

General information: 415.561.4900

Getting There: Visiting Alcatraz requires a ferry ride; visit www.parksconservancy.org or call 415.981.7625 for ticket costs and trip times.

Look For:
- Cellhouse
- Island nature
- Military history
- Historic gardens

Activities: Cellhouse audio tour, exhibits, nature walk, short documentary on the 1969-1971 occupation of Alcatraz by Native Americans, ranger-led programs, museum store

Tips: Alcatraz is directly in line with the Golden Gate, and fog and cold ocean breezes are the norm; dress accordingly.

	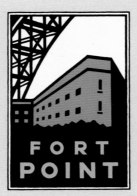	
FORT MASON	**FORT POINT**	**THE PRESIDIO**
General information: 415.561.4700 (TTD/V, 556.2766)	General information: 415.556.1693 (TDD, 561.4399)	General information: 415.561.4323 (TTY, 561.4314)
In San Francisco: Bay Street to Franklin; Franklin ends in Fort Mason.	Fort Point is tucked under the south anchorage of the Golden Gate Bridge; take Lincoln Boulevard or Mason Street (through Crissy Field) and watch for signs directing you to the access road.	On the tip of the San Francisco peninsula; numerous access points (Lombard ends in the Presidio, and Highway 1 passes through it).
• Aquatic Park • Black Point Battery • Fort Mason Center • Great Meadow • Marina Green • Park Headquarters and Pacific West Information Center	• Civil War-era fort • Golden Gate Bridge • Dramatic waves	• Baker Beach • Crissy Field and Crissy Field Center • Fort Scott • Lobos Creek • Main Post • San Francisco National Cemetery • Native plant nursery
Walking in the Great Meadow and along the Golden Gate Promenade, which begins in nearby Aquatic Park; museums and restaurants in Fort Mason Center	Fort tours, ranger-led programs, self-guided audio tour, films on the building of the bridge and history of the fort, wildflowers (in season)	Walking, jogging, hiking, biking, ranger-led programs, environmental education programs for children and families, sailboarding
Watch—and listen—for wild parrots overhead; a flock of these noisy, bright green birds spends much of its time in Fort Mason.	The Pacific Ocean and the San Francisco Bay meet under the Golden Gate Bridge, and it's usually windy and often cool here; dress accordingly.	The Presidio, under the joint supervision of the National Park Service and the Presidio Trust, is home to a number of environmentally focused organizations; inquire at the Visitor Center for more information.

	SUTRO HEIGHTS	FORT FUNSTON	SWEENEY RIDGE
PARK	 **SUTRO HEIGHTS** General information: 415.561.4323	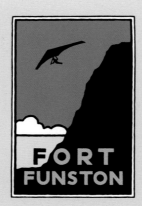 **FORT FUNSTON** General information: 415.561.4323	 **SWEENEY RIDGE** General information: 415.561.4323
GETTING THERE	In San Francisco; entrance at 48th Avenue and Point Lobos, on the ocean side of the San Francisco Peninsula.	Take the Great Highway south from the Cliff House area; watch for signs directing you to the entrance to Fort Funston.	Take Skyline Boulevard/Highway 35; look for Sharp Park Road (Milagra Ridge), College Drive (Sweeney Ridge), and the town of Woodside on Highway 280 (Phleger Estate).
LOOK FOR	• Cliff House • Lands End • Ocean Beach • Sutro Bath ruins • Sutro Heights • USS *San Francisco* Memorial • West Fort Miley picnic area	• Coastal and paved trails • Hang gliding platform • Native plant nursery • Thornton Beach State Park	• Portola Expedition Memorial • Milagra Ridge • Phleger Estate • Sweeney Ridge • Mori Point
ACTIVITIES	Walking, hiking, beachwalking, birdwatching, shipwreck-spotting, ranger-led programs	Hang-gliding, hiking, beachwalking, equestrian, wildflowers (in season) ranger-led programs	Hiking, birdwatching, wildflowers (in season)
TIPS	A popular segment of the Coastal Trail runs through this area, but be aware that the cliffs are unstable—stay on the trail.	Fort Funston is a Hang-III (intermediate) site with a launch area and wheelchair-accessible viewing deck.	These areas, also called the Watershed lands, offer different but equally appealing experiences. At the Phleger Estate, you can walk in a second-growth redwood forest, while Sweeney and Milagra ridges offer great bay views. Mori Point is a dramatic promontory.

ABOUT THE CONTRIBUTORS

Space limitations preclude a full listing of the contributors' career highlights. Look for them on the Internet, or write to the publisher for more information on how to contact them. The Golden Gate National Parks Conservancy is extremely appreciative of the courtesies extended by these individuals.

The Author

CHRISTINE COLASURDO (San Francisco, CA) is a frequently published nature writer, member of the California Native Plant Society, and (with her husband and son) an inveterate hiker. Her book, *Return to Spirit Lake: Journey Through a Lost Landscape*, examines the May 18, 1980, eruption of Mount St. Helens and its consequences.

The Photographers

ROB BADGER (Marin City, CA) has photographed the beauty of the earth and its accelerating destruction for 35 years, winning international awards for his Antarctica series and "best in journalism" for his evocative environmental photography. robbadger@excelonline.com

ROY EISENHARDT (San Francisco, CA), whose work illustrates the book, *Gardens of Alcatraz*, has photographed the parks extensively over a period of many years. Formerly executive director of the California Academy of Sciences, he has traveled widely in pursuit of his photographic avocation.

MACDUFF EVERTON (Santa Barbara, CA) is a fine art photographer represented by Janet Borden Inc., NYC, at 212.431.0166. www.macduffeverton.com

RICHARD FREAR is a National Park Service photographer.

JEFF GNASS (Juneau, AK), who specializes in large-format photographs of scenic and natural history subjects, has accumulated thousands of photo credits in a wide variety of books, calendars, and major magazines. www.jeffgnass.com

AL GREENING (San Francisco, CA) works with both panoramic and 35 mm cameras. A docent at Point Bonita Lighthouse since 1985, he has conducted many photo walks in the Marin Headlands. algreening@msn.com

INGER HOGSTROM (Oakland, CA) is a stock photographer whose work has been published nationally and internationally. Fine art prints of her work are included in collections across the country. www.ingerhogstrom.com

KERRICK JAMES (Mesa, AZ) has been photographing the American West and Mexico for more than twenty years, with increasing emphasis on Alaska, Hawaii, and Baja California. His work has appeared on more than sixty covers and feature stories in travel and inflight magazines. www.kerrickjames.com

DAVID JESUS (Danville, CA), whose work has been published in educational materials, journals, and newspapers, is also an avid birdwatcher and volunteer with the Golden Gate Raptor Observatory in the Marin Headlands. RaptorPictures@aol.com

CHARLES KENNARD (San Anselmo, CA) is the photographer and author of *San Francisco Bay Area Landmarks*. A native of England, he has a special interest in traditional uses of plants, is active in habitat restoration work, and often leads photo walks in the parks.

GARY KRAMER (Willows, CA) has had work published in numerous books, national magazines, and calendars. Before retiring in 1999, he had a 26-year career as a biologist/refuge manager with the US Fish and Wildlife Service. www.garykramer.net

MINDY MANVILLE (Davis, CA) has documented many of the Golden Gate National Parks during her photographic career.

JED MANWARING (Novato, CA), a professional location photographer, specializes in nature, landscapes, and people. His photographs have been published in magazines, calendars, cards, and advertising. www.jedmanwaring.com

MARC MUENCH (Goleta, CA) has been a professional landscape and sports photographer since 1989. Now president of Muench Photography, Inc., he continues to add to the Muench Photography collection. His photographic specialty is incorporating people into the landscape. www.muenchphotography.com

EMILY NEWBY (Arcata, CA), a naturalist, monitored the endangered mission blue and San Bruno elfin butterflies at Milagra Ridge in 1999 and 2000.

GALEN ROWELL (Bishop, CA), internationally known as a photographer, writer, and mountaineer, has spent the last three decades photographing the world's high and wild places. Fine prints, books, workshops, assignments, and stock photography are available through Mountain Light Photography. www.mountainlight.com

BARBARA SAMUELSON (Alameda, CA) has traveled throughout western North America, from Alaska to Mexico, photographing wildlife and the outdoors. www.barbarascamera.com

DAVID SANGER (Albany, CA) is a widely published photojournalist who has photographed for numerous travel magazines and environmental organizations. His photography book on San Francisco Bay will be published by U of California Press. www.davidsanger.com

DENNIS SHERIDAN (Los Osos, CA) is a native Californian who has traveled world-wide photographing nature, with a concentration on birds of prey and native wildlife as well as fungi, lichens, insects, and wildflowers. dennissher@thegrid.net

BRENDA THARP (Novato, CA) specializes in outdoor and travel photographs, which appear in a variety of national magazines, book publishers, and environmental organizations. www.brendatharp.com

LARRY ULRICH (Trinidad, CA) and his wife Donna—his chief field critic—have published a number of books, including volumes with Companion Press and Chronicle Books. Since 1972, they have traveled more than half the year in search of images for their stock photo collection. www.larryulrich.com

BARON WOLMAN (Santa Fe, NM), *Rolling Stone*'s first chief photographer, is also a widely published aerial photographer. www.fotobaron.com